POETICEXPRESSIONISM

POETICEXPRESSIONISM

BY

CHARLES WILLIAMS

Copyright © 2016 Charles K. Williams
All rights reserved.

ISBN: 0692689672
ISBN-13: 978-0-692-68967-7

Solsinmotion, first Edition

Copyright © 2016 by Charles K. Williams

All Rights reserved under International and Pan-American Copyright conventions, including the right of reproduction in whole or part in any form.

No part of this book may be reproduced or utilized in any form or by any means, electronic or mechanical, including photocopying, recording, or by any information storage or retrieval system, without permission in writing from the author. Inquiries should be addressed to: Solsinmotion, P.O. BOX #365, Santa Monica, CA 90401

Library of Congress Cataloging-in-Publication Data
Williams, Charles K
[Poems, selections]

ISBN: 978-0-692-68967-7 (PAPERBACK)
ISBN-10: 0692689672

Book Cover design by Anna Huff

Manufactured in The United States of America

DEDICATION

This book is dedicated to all those who have impacted my life and left behind a legacy of love, inspiration, and affection that I am forever thankful for. Each one of you have made a significant impact in my life and I am truly blessed to be able to keep your memory alive. I want to thank my grandmother, Lelieth Douglas, my uncles: Winston Miller, Cornelius Dunkley, Berris Cunningham, my best friend, Jomo Francis, and my father figure: Lester "Lucky" McBride. This is also for my mom who has sacrificed, worked hard, and dedicated her life to see me thrive and live my life to the fullest. I also want to thank my dad Nathanial Williams. In addition I want to thank Robert L. Waller, my friend, brother, and editor of this book. Also, in addition I want to thank Anna Huff for designing the book cover, and Eric Morago for being my other pair of format editing eyes. Plus, my brother Nathaniel Williams who recorded and edited the audiobook. I have nothing but love for all my family, friends and everyone who I have come in contact with.

POETICEX TABLE OF CONCEPTS

0. Step Into A World

Neurogenics: journey through my mind: pg. 10

I. TRUE OR FALSE (Stories)

What to say: pg. 12

Damage: pg. 15

Woman scorned: pg. 18

Never seen a man cry: pg. 21

Lost and found: pg. 22

Extra Extra: pg. 24

She wanted: pg. 26

Impressionable: pg. 28

Supa-Star: pg. 29

Happiness: pg. 32

On my block: pg. 35

Another night on the roof: pg. 39

II. DIGGING DEEP (Inspiration)

I am: pg. 42

On The Road Again: pg. 43

Passion: pg. 44

Foresight: pg. 45

Incarcerated: pg. 46

A lull: pg. 47

Turn me up: pg. 48

Worldview: pg. 50

No hypotheticals: pg. 51

Sincerity: pg. 54

A penny for my thoughts: pg. 55

Father: pg. 58

III. SOCIAL LANDSCAPE (Sociopolitical)

The Black KKK: pg. 60

If they only knew: pg. 62

Feel me: pg. 63

Righteous way to go: pg. 65

Be this way: pg. 66

Mask: pg. 68

Double-sided: pg. 69

Going through the motions: pg. 71

The voice of a capitalist: pg. 73

Death of a salesman: pg. 76

For my people: pg. 79

Innocence lost: pg. 81

IV. OUTER PLANETARY (Existentialism)

Tempo: pg. 84

After dark: pg. 86

A gamble: pg. 87

A mother's nature: pg. 88

Cyclical: pg. 89

Bandwidth: pg. 90

The city of angels: pg. 91

It's over: pg. 93

Nothing: pg. 94

Acid rain: pg. 95

El sole: pg. 96

Float on: pg. 98

V. LOVEY DOVEY (Romance)

More than you know: pg. 102

Sweet music: pg. 105

Wish: pg. 106

Rebirth: pg. 107

Band-Aid: pg. 108

Seasons: pg. 109

Much more: pg. 111

Going blind: pg. 113

Evidence: pg. 114

All good: pg. 117

A piece of: pg. 118

Breakthrough: pg. 120

POETICEXPRESSIONISM: GLOSSARY: pg. 121

ABOUT THE AUTHOR: pg. 122

STEP INTO A WORLD

.0.

Neurogenics: Journey Through My Mind

Poeticexpressionism is a collection of poems that I have compiled to give the reader an idea of the multiple electro-charges that spark my synapses that transmogrify into thoughts. We have over 50,000-70,000 thoughts per day, according to the National Science Foundation. This means between 35 and 48 thoughts per minute per person. However, it did take a lot of thought to write, compile and edit each poem. Somehow, through infinite possibility, these thoughts metamorphosed into a book. So please wear a multi-dimensional mind when reading because each piece is a world within a world within a world. It is my honor to share my world with you, the reader.

We all have shared experiences that connect us on all levels, and this book is one of them. The level we'll be traveling on can't be comprehended by thought alone, but with the inclusion of feeling. Each and every thought is super charged and magnified through feeling. The feeling itself is carried by energy.

Thoughts without intention are like balloons without helium; they will not float anywhere. Each piece travels on its own and takes you somewhere. Though, that somewhere is for you the reader to decide. I do not hold myself responsible for the outcome of what occurs after reading this book because that is not my responsibility. My responsibility is to share and convey the messages that were inputted into me by a greater Source. By Source I mean where all things originate in my humble opinion. This book is written truly on inspiration.

I am only collecting my thoughts in this moment. For all we have are moments and memories. Moments are fleeting and memories can last a lifetime. And as I live out my moment in time, my thoughts will last a lifetime. There is no denying that in the ether all was, all is and all will be. I choose to be present in the now with my thoughts. If you dare to join me, please be present in mine and yours because your awareness allows me to join with you as well. Interconnectedness is the best, more or less we all coalesce in the spirit and the flesh. LETS GO!!!

TRUE OR FALSE
I

WHAT TO SAY

It really doesn't matter what I came up here to tell you

I could say anything

anything

talk about nothing and make it sound like something

recycle topics,

rekindle their relevancy

make a lie sound sweet

and the truth hard to swallow

speak of known knowns

unknown knowns

known unknowns,

but what I know

is that for whatever I tell you

you make it mean what it means

I got no control over that

because words don't have power without intention

otherwise they're just words

we give words meaning

that meaning reinforced by feeling

Therefore

it matters how I say it

how I communicate

how it resonates inside of you

the emotions that ensue

this isn't anything new

acknowledged the moment I stepped up here

might as well been naked

we both in it for the connection

discard the act

let's face our vulnerability together

I can admit I'm scared

scared if I don't perform

what if I freeze up

and you scared I might do the same

but I feel we both want the same

you want me to touch you in places that resemble home

make you uncomfortably comfortable

converse with your thoughts

speak life into your dreams

trigger your anger for injustice

insinuate your fire for freedom

soul burning bright blue

unleash tears of sorrow

that feed the soil of your mind

growing into meadows of joy

tap into your hunger for knowledge

your thirst for something pure

take you way out there

thinking I might leave you

but genuinely believe I will bring you back safe

have recess in the deep recesses of your mind

have your heart attack your throat

because it's choked up with love

beat sense into your consciousness

passive and aggressive

your martyr for honesty

wear truth like a crown of thorns

bleed art

onto the palette of your imagination

paint vivid stories

of the past, present, future

to immortalize the now

where we exist together

moment fleeting

memory vine repeating

I could have been your first

your in-between

or your last

but you'll be hard to forget

this experience

because

it's not what I said

                        But how I said it

DAMAGE

I see you

in I.C.U.

for the wrong you thought to do

you and your makeshift crew planned a coup

but there was a miscue

a minor issue

that all along I knew

from the start

what is in the light came out of the dark

couldn't play your part

you were my heart

tried outsmarting your counterpart

Superman you weren't Clark

my senses keen

instincts sharp

from the start

I knew

the time you were going to depart

when your plan was to commence

this was going to be my swan song

you were thoroughly convinced

however your honesty rested in disloyalty

unabridged arrogance

spread like cheap liquor store incense

my sixth sense picked up your foul stench like a hound

watching as all your lackeys gathered around

proclaiming tonight is the night you claim the crown

I stared and frowned

more or less I was astounded

anger arose

but I stayed grounded

didn't let my emotions get the best of me

the sad reality

my ally is my enemy

knowing there could have been a possibility

but I had to see it for myself

didn't want to hear it from anyone else's mouth but him

can't deny it now no matter his explanation

he wanted my resignation

in his anticipation

never knew what was waiting for him

a counter attack of disproportionate proportions

no more horsing

since he wanted his brother in a coffin

I knew Cane was able

all those nights he ate at my table

chilled at my home

a salacious traitor

the epitome of a *hater* gunning for my throne

as if I would not have known,

but to his surprise

when he got to the gate

he was surrounded by a couple of my guys

tried talking,

but I told him no more lies

I see it in your eyes

your despise

wanting my demise

the chance to sodomize my kingdom

making everyone your minions

the audacity to think of disgracing Mr. Williams

and all he built

threatening if my name is mentioned

then that person would be killed

feeling so betrayed

but this is the bed he made

I won't send him to an early grave

but somewhere remote to suffer

for wanting to execute his brother

jealousy can make anyone a slave

and temptation can easily become your lover

WOMAN SCORNED

There's nothing like hearing

Donna and Karen swearing

blaring out stories of childbearing

the designer clothes they children wearing

speak so loud both hard of hearing

attention seeking

temperatures flaring

phat booty Gucci jump suits

dookie earrings

cold staring

eyes glaring

smearing each other's names

they Kobe and LeBron James

every day the playoffs

they both want them *rangs*

shinny *thangs*

playing mind games

in designer frames

going mid-evil like Ving Rhames

no pulp in their fiction

they gulp disdain

can't count accountability

stuck on blame

doing the same old same

what a shame

think they both right

when they both to blame

Aim--white strip
locked behind Colgate
spandex--tight fit
breath fresh of hate
jealousy in their veins
ready to shank one another like convicts
control freaks, dominatrix
stay broke
hair and nails fixed
affixed on their crucifix
of sex, revenge, and desire
the basics to snag the men they require
turning gold digging into an occupation
Karrine Steffans they admire
their super head is hot fire, blazing
scheming to get ahead
indicted on the same priors
their admirers
unaware of these liars
selling their love traps to the highest buyers
now Bob is on the wires
Ty is under the tires
until their charge cards expire
scandalous and they proud of it too
can't tell them any different
they put the I in *ignant* and indignant
their imaginations are figment cookies
fallen rose petals and crooked stairs to grace

their eyes are windows to nowhere

and souls sandpaper bare

exploitation is tatted on their face

hearts have a sign that say beware

no playing fair

ain't no rules to war

humanity has disappeared

they will die for Vuitton and Couture

no minks speared

what for

when they letting their suitors hit it raw

entrap them like *Saw*

they both Jigsaw

wearing the same masks

gave up on reality a long time ago

their lives clash like *Crash* for cash

they compared and contrast

prepared with trash bags

to snag sugar-dads and lads for laughs

how sad that their present future remains in the past

old broads looking young like Stacey Dash

if the price is right

anyone can smash

NEVER SEEN A MAN CRY

Why is he crying

did someone give him something to cry about

men aren't suppose to shed tears

been told that for years

that real men have no fears

they have no business being scared

and it's weak to display emotion

Shoulders built broad

to support everyone

but himself

legs stout

feet rooted in earth

spine straight

neck firm

conditioned to withstand pressure

but pressure builds within

Heart tangled like misdirected vines

thoughts lost in grey matter

tornados

stomach anxiously erupting

volcanoes

a man buried under the implosion

of false expectations

to drown in a sea of his own tears

LOST AND FOUND

The bottled up feelings of disgust

severed connections of trust

she wants to adjust

but for years been hurt

to many games been played

been tugged into a war that has left her jerked

she walks around aimlessly

thinking the world is out to get her

thinking it'll forget her

not at ease

won't settle

until placed in mortuary

acts as if she is not scared

but horrified by life's possibilities

always weary and borderline

useless at best

existence null and void

denial of her sacred

avoids human contact

standing in dead space

with her back against a wall

no one to call or converse with

murders self-esteem daily

double jeopardy

pleads the fifth

never been told she's precious

never received any love letters

represses dreams

strangles imagination

can't tell her nothing

carves lies into skin

countless attempts at suicide

believes she's a failure

couldn't kill herself when she tried

sleeps with eyes wide open

thoughts stampeding

keeping her awake

the pain runs deep

the tears soak the sheets

hunger is elusive

rarely eats

scathed voice obtrusive

barely speaks

walks while dead

but her heart still beats

EXTRA EXTRA

Got back from the battlefield

paradise lost

river of broken dreams revealed

how am I to deal

how am I to heal

dates involved face to face conversations with the steel

witness to lives being stolen

death is omnipresent

there's no time to feel

or they'll ask your family if they want the casket closed or open

plenty of petty promises broken

dreams wiped with tattered rags of blood soaking

holding guilt like a plate of waits

I killed forty-four times during my two tours

crazy eighty-eights

our platoon doomed from the start of the war

most never reached shore

storming on the hour glass beaches of Normandy

sand storms swirl in a disconcerting Afghan orgy

broadcasts are forgeries

nothing glamorous in hearing the cries of dying men

inappropriate to show senseless brutality

the daily casualties multiply and divide nations

we fighting for your freedom

a free market system

but our freedom is under siege

we're AWOL on these missions,

but accessories include fatigues and a M63
loaded with the hate that breeds destruction
for the mass consumption of economic resources
label these patriots of corruption remorseless
they send in additional forces
to force out the opposition and put in new bosses
while maintaining production to prevent capital losses
modern day Crusades and we bearing the crosses
I've seen the four horses and the men riding them
they tell me my time will come
but until then
that's when I'll dance with death
and I'm not the type to be brash,
but I asked God why
is this church
the Holy Ghost seems to make frequent visits
when these soldiers throw their arms to the sky
screaming your name before they die
here in a sec.
then gone in a blink of an eye

SHE WANTED

She wanted to dance

but she felt trapped by circumstances

the pressure to live up to her father and mother's ideals

She wanted to sing

but the fear of ridicule kept her mouth sealed

a voice trapped inside

a soul at the great divide

where truth and lies coincide

She wanted to be

but didn't want to pay the price to be free

standing motionless on the inside

the caged bird locked in captivity

IMPRESSIONABLE

There is a contingent of scrupulous scribes

who write with their tongues cut out

stuck up their ass

because they're always talking shit

And of course they think their shit don't stink

they've become all too familiar with the smell and taste

compulsively loathing

lathering and soaking in

in thoughts that are broken

provoking impressionable minds

by masking and cloaking

behind grand designs of

white lines

Coked up

fashionable

Cold cuts

not amicable

Rolled up

their lectures

Hannibal

Hold up

their rhetoric

can eat a dick

dictation irrational

And I don't fashion myself after the mass-produced
outsourced
under-resourced
brokeback mountain racehorse
ending up on the defensive
in courts of public opinion

This piece is for all my children
whose futures resemble attrition
today there's a restriction on original thinking
art programs are shrinking
self-preservation is sinking
integrity is hitting rock bottom

Therefore I solemnly swear
to approach my love transparently
holding poetry near and dear to my heart
close for comfort
always on point
sharp
permanent like birthmark
symbiosis of art and soul
Descartes
rejecting any appeals to an end

SUPA-STAR

I'm through with the hard acting *cats*

talking about gats

how they mack while counting stacks

that's fine and dandy

ceremoniously live it in their raps

only bold when hitting caps

the facts

plagiarize felonious acts on tracks

then turn around and be sweet like candy

not a fan *B*

not even giving them the time of day

don't care if they didn't hear me

clearly this message goes out to all

pride besets the fall

as low as they are

no room to crawl

anatomically incorrect Ken doll

missing vital parts

like for one

heart

the other skills

making yourself a target

that's why you a *mark*

putting yourself in uncomfortable situations

nothing but talk Rex Ryan

false expectations

now you jet

looking for relief

your ambition as a rider

only lasts as long as you take Viagra

A side show act

abracadabra

an actor

a combination of Bow-Wow and Hannah Montana

your punch lines and witty *banta*

colorful like Fanta

a sore on the game

canker

bloody wanker

the quintessential Fisher Price my first toolkit

screwing yourself all your life

thought you could do it the music

subconsciously therapeutic

forcing yourself onto something that loved you

more than you knew what to do with

attached yourself like a crab

in the area of the pubics

a good reason for DJ's to scratch

sometimes when you turn on a track

ignorance is the worst disease you can catch

I know you're complex

not your rhyme structure

let me put this into context

you herpes

a hazardous waste symbol sits on your album cover

Please get *gutta*

gully

and *grimy*

call your entourage

and tell them to come find me

I'll be standing on the corner of legal and action

I know your people

they'll kill me when they're rapping

that's the only time they get it cracking

only for platinum

their anthem:

I pledge allegiance to the fake MC

one nation without God

checks with lots of decibels

with big booty freaks

clothing lines

and hood movies for all,

World Star

a bunch of Harold and Kumars

impossible to perceive that they're real *sun*

they talk real dumb

ain't nothing real from them

the sad thing is if they came real

then hip-hop would have given them the rhythm

now they can talk that hard stuff in prison

while getting that hard stuff

they'll adjust nicely to their new conditions

HAPPINESS

Been feeling lost for years
a stranger amongst my pairs
although my family says they love me
still feel like they don't care

Am I empty inside
feelings clouded in cyanide
dueling with duality
drove me to this divide

I'd rather spend my time alone
locked in my room at home
arms zipper slit
to use my blood to write love poems

And even if I was the last man on earth
that wouldn't reverse this sensation of being cursed
it would still feel like life went from bad to worse
because I would still ask why wasn't I the first one gone

Never borderline depression
I was its full expression
Prozac, Lithium, Valium consumed
intravenous digestion of therapeutic suggestion
that thwarted hope into further repression

Now where do I have to go
on this endless ride in vertigo
spinning round and round merry-go
ain't nothing Mary, but I hope she hear me
please tell your son to perform them same miracles
like he and his disciples did in the Bible

I'm likeable but that don't mean I like you too
I'm liable to go off the deep end
why have friends
when each second could be the end
a never endless cycle of maniacal suicidal thinking

Really don't need a reason no more
what for
explain myself--shame myself
in the same place I was before

This war been going on since
and it don't make sense
the rage and incense
only wanted to be held

Well I guess they could tell
when they inspect my neck
and see the rope imprints
welcome to a living hell

All that it is cracked up to be

darkness and despair decorates my mental cell

wishful thinking could have been better

but this was the life for me

ON MY BLOCK

On my block
me and boys were young jocks

playing ball non-stop

fell in love with hip-hop

90's Cross Colors, Timbs, Jordans, G-Shocks

we had no concept of time

forget a watch

family use sign language for us to come in for din-din

run inside eat

then come back on the block to play again

We were restless

no resting

reckless wrestling

always messing around

wasn't stressing

that was a foreign concept

dead weights only good for lifting

so we lifted inanimate objects

envisioned our faces on top decks

girls and sex

we teens what you expect

fights for respect

when other crews would step

back then could catch a fair one

now *cats* unload clips like a 20 pack of lit cigarettes

quick to pull a gun

we want to make it to the kingdom
but we'll take our time to come
now some of us have daughters and sons
a family we're *raise-un*

"But back in the days when we were young,
but we're not kids anymore,
but some days I sit and wish we were kids again"

Reminiscing when we got around
on the electric relaxation
blazing on the cronic
getting illmattic
because we were ready to die
93 till infinity,
but she kept passing us by
time got a way of doing that
continuous A-track
history repeats itself
lapse

Trips down memory lane on your brain's train tracks
neighborhood scare of anthrax or Unabomber
Jessie ran for president in '88
now yes we can Obama
poppas and mommas telling us
we can be what we want to be
play the game

hurdle the racial barrier in our society

although the rights were civil

the Right didn't display civility

drugs ran rampant in our communities

drug war

now they're more black men in jail than all of slavery

L.A. riots an example of the disparity

can't pardon the parody

Fab Five established a cultural identity

bald head, black socks, Huaraches

media called them thugs

then us black youth were carbon copies

always made to be the outsider

until we became N.W.A riders

something must have got inside us

because we became freedom fighters

wore our hearts on our sleeves

sleeves burning on fire

Tired of being cut off

no love lost

because a racial divide had to be crossed

cost not a factor

experience cannot be quantified

#Blacklivesmatter

remembering all those that died

that tried to make our lives better

told us to never say never

and have some pride

most of all have fun enjoy the ride

on my block

ANOTHER NIGHT ON THE ROOF

Staring down on the city

on top of a metropolitan Mount Olympus

observations bear witness

to the *sadity* like Diddy

or the *gritty* like Fifty

indulging their self interest

in a fictitious popularity contest

there is a populace residing in Gotham's palace

intrinsically bearing the burden of scorn

cursing the day they were born

these eagles nest in the bosom of thorns

growing into terrorists

conclusions drawn forlorn

if you can't fly

falling,

it's so long

the inherent harm

of not being warned

can't set off the internal alarm

muting the champion sound

could of have been undisputed

now they're ignorant of their nature

from being uprooted

looted for their intrinsic value

heading to the Crypt because they bled Piru

on 575 Haiku Avenue

lives paraphrased to fit an ad

most don't have a clue
where to get their poetic license
if it were common
then everyone would have common sense
that's why most subscribe to artificial intelligence
their thought process is filled with junk mail
irrelevance
remnants of their past selves
watered down
when they use to be bright as pastels
lumped up like camels
not giving a damn
violence and sex sells
reaching for heaven
but locked themselves in hells cells
after eating hells bells
their set dipped like Hell Rell
trapped in the closet like Kells
searching for precious like the Hobbit
can't avoid turning into Smeagles
how unfortunate the state of the peoples
the evils
being fed intravenously with needles
the position they're in
fetal
Another night in the city

DIGGING DEEP
II

I AM

I am hard to describe

I am not to be categorized

I am many things to many people

I am the cause and effect of many lives

I am the many of eyes that have seen me rise like the Phoenix

I am right the first time without having to make the remix

I am like the helix a constant

I am a bold C consonant

I am enough content to fill up a whole continent

I am never content

I am everyday making heroic attempts

I am pushing myself to the furthest extent

I am taking what is irrelevant and throwing it away

I am taking what is relevant and using it every day

I am supplanting pretentious preponderance for positive prevalence

I am speaking in prose that are oh so eloquent

I am on another plateau

I am sentient

ON THE ROAD AGAIN

I'm honoring my decision

to live in my own skin

guiding my steps

two feet will not be a walking contradiction

on the path of hypocrisy

I've mastered my profession as a physician

took the Hippocratic Oath

to be of service with utmost integrity

because everyday my humanity is on display

like a Salvador Dali resting in the Guggenheim

I'm a portrait of the surreal

a contemporary for exemplary appeal

charm, grace, ingenuity

Along my nerve endings I feel, calm, safe, security

knowing that I am receiving the affection I need

to thrive in a world that dissects its insecurities

suffocating in its lack of self-esteem

numbing the possibility of conscious thought

only to be conditioned by suggestive reasoning

suggesting that the only reliable reason is to safeguard perspective

PASSION

Have you ever felt passionate

giving your all

even when you had nothing left

your last dime

your last breath

to see it wash away and come back again

to stand out on the edge of darkness

not knowing if the light will ever shine again

but only a faint glimmer appears with a dull sparkle

wondering when will it return

and your heart burns

yearning for that feeling once more

knowing the essence of what you and it could become

a life full of wonder and amazement

there is nothing to replace the void

but in the distance there is a faint sound

FORESIGHT

Today is your day to remember

do not lock it in a box

keep it exposed

uncontained

let us process your process

you took the road less taken

and seldom followed

with confidence and cunning

recognizing the task at hand

you set out and achieved

accomplished your mission

you are an inspiration to us all

for you saw the I in you

where others would see none

INCARCERATED

The greatest crime committed against mankind

is the crime against the mind

we've been lied to so much

that the truth is an anomalous paradigm

can't discern the two

that reality becomes a riddled blurred line

therefore it's up to you to find

THE TRUTH

A LULL

This is a period--point break

The childish things I did

the imagination of how I lived fades and dissipates

making it big

the only dream I had as a kid

put on hold to wait

adolescent crisis fueling the debate

will I change if I get older

the taste of caviar not my caveat

much more of root beer float type of guy

built my house on a rock above sand castles

when the ground drops far from frazzled

saw the light

dazzled,

reached out

grappled,

took a bite out the apple of continuity

tackling the dualism of duality

locked inside a time capsule

preserving fresh conserved fragments

flying like a bird caught in the tight grasps of the wind

in the air of my ear making sure I heard

the only urge that needs to be satisfied

is peace in my sleep

in my sleep when I die

a quiet lull to lulling my lullaby

TURN ME UP

Battling with insomnia

staring incessantly at this paper

comalike symptoms

words swirling in my head

constant,

trying to write a story of a lifetime

no one in particular

only mine

can't even conceptualize the first line

going in reverse

to find the story line

then all of a sudden

the sunshine hits my pupil

a mercurial rainbow appears

sweet music to my ears

the pen lifts to conduct a musical

without me switching chairs

nearly bursting into tears

overcome with raw sanguine emotion

hand in motion

jet propulsion

thoughts coasting

releasing gratitude that harbors inside

shedding away pride

letting the real me out

outside

scope wide

vision unlimited

faults magnified

vulnerability exhibited

writing is spirited

perspective uninhibited

experience can't be discredited

uncensored

unedited

uplifted

WORLDVIEW

We in it together

no one is excused

Christians

Muslims

Jews

Buddhists

Hindus

and any other religious groups

I didn't include

NO HYPOTHETICALS

If you can keep your head

when all about you are losing theirs

not succumb to your fears

take the lumps over the years

wipe away the seasonal tears

cuz a new day is coming

you ain't seen nothing yet

good things come to those who wait

what you're bound to get is worth its weight in gold

food for the soul

forthcoming and foretold

written in scripture

all you had to get was the picture

before your destiny could get with *yah*

crack it like a Swisher

isn't she sweet

reaping what you sow

appreciate being at your peak

coming up from below

slow isn't imperative

watching yourself grow is where it is

you only got one life to live

most aren't born privileged

still no excuse not to cross that bridge

to experience the exquisite

the finer things

persistence pays for the inquisitive

the reward that hard work brings

permanent mood swing

excess melting away

like losing that gut

P90x couldn't get you this cut

hard body

flexible mind

resounding spirit

when motivation struck

it wasn't luck

you hustled

moved your butt

Jaws of life saved you

unstuck

lined your ambitions in order

saved pennies and quarters

no more hors d'oeuvres

you can have anything the menu offers

everything else is for the birds

in the end you get what you deserve

self-preservation

you were meant to sit at the table

already had reservations

far exceeding your expectations

blow out the candles

enjoy the celebration

it's your party tonight

for your amalgamation

Congratulations!

SINCERITY

I give it up to anyone putting themselves out there
there is anywhere they feel
feeling their dreams with their own two hands
hands that wait for thought and feeling to connect
the ones who disconnect the life support
when there is no support
the only support comes in the form of judgment,
judgment from friends and family
too scared to live theirs,
but I always admire those that step out on theirs
knowing there is an endless supply of foresight
for their sight is reliable and trustworthy,
worthy to receive the fruits of their labor always,
always putting yourself out there when you want something
for that something
take the risk
the risk of getting your head chopped off
clean off in front of everyone
for not everyone can handle the burden of ridicule
because ridicule is the burden of genius

A PENNY FOR MY THOUGHTS

A penny for my thoughts

no,

my thoughts are priceless

can't be bought

but I'll share them with those in conscious crisis

value of self in the minus

thoughts are gold

Midas

Big, small, all different sizes

what you need

food for thought that *appetises* your cerebral cortex

feeling it down to your solar plexus

deep within your nexus

draw pluses from X's

traveling inside spiritual vortexes

your world spinning positively on its axis

gaining further access into your being

seeing that your existence has meaning

now you know hu-man is leading

returning to the Garden of Eden

don't have to die to meet God

the Divine Spirit inside keeps your heart beating

living in a state of happiness is true heaven on earth

since your birth your mind has been convoluted

polluted with false ideals

suppose to keep you on your toes

but most trained to heel

beg, borrow, steal and even kill

what happened to free will

you have the right to choose

can live a life of abundance or play the blues

the duality of win and lose is repeatedly overused

abused when playing by man's rules

who is left to reap the rewards of tragedy

the victim's family

stop the insanity

plan-A ain't working

try plan-B

generosity and sincerity

on the back of black streets

light shines infinitely

unraveling the secrecy of mystery

cogitate unequivocally

beyond the 33rd degree

freer than masonry

you are Sacred Geometry

tap into your supercharged energy fields

if seeing is believing

then the things unseen wouldn't be real

we also have to feel

release your intuition

thoughts matching your experience of volition

let yourself go

give yourself permission

go on your expedition to find your life's true purpose

break underneath the surface

you are valuable and desirable

opposite of worthless

highly favored and blessed

without going to churches

if you step forward

the process of conditioning reverses

permanently

FATHER

I was lucky

to have known a man

who didn't plant this seed

but nurtured another man's garden,

hands dug in dirt

palms calloused from the labor of love

but still gentile enough to uplift this young soul,

made sure I knew my roots

instructed me on how to stand firm

not only by words

but example

treated me like his own

and I can still hear him call me son

he was my sun

standing directly above me

with smile shining like 10,000 galaxies

there is no track of time

only stardust

glimmering in my eyes

soul transitioned into the great beyond,

say hi to Grandma

keep her company

the same way you kept me

the same way I keep you in my heart,

however it was fate

destiny

to call another man father

SOCIAL LANDSCAPE
III

THE BLACK KKK

Now you asking--who's this black KKK

the same lost brothers who let their AK's spray

momma crying hey for her *bay-bay*

because another brother took his life away

could say we an endangered species

kill our selves off faster than a disease

please we's been cut off at the ankle

now resting on our knees

but "real" *G's* be's dying for unowned street properties

fighting for gang territories

haven't read none of Booker T's philosophies

on seizing job opportunities

building for their families

going after degrees

scholarly pursuits

Instead looking like apes and brutes

enslaving minds like in *Roots*

feeding regurgitated poison to the youth

Won't make any apologies

for addressing the inadequacies of the human species

the ones that specifically believe in inequities

discriminate against their disparities

a false sense of entitlement

arrogant tendencies

the evident evidence of ignorance grows like weeds

prisoners to their insecurities

Chains chiseled with grooves of compassion

they can break out of the boundaries of repression

the preponderance of perpetual character extinction

to never see the road to perdition

IF THEY ONLY KNEW

Some won't ever get it

that's ok

they can have the synthetics

alcohol and prescription drugs

keeping it 100 is a Naturalist's code of ethics

one love

don't mess with genetically modified buds

scientists say its fine the way it is

in actuality

it's good the way it was

FEEL ME

Years spent in seclusion

believe we're owed restitution

for breathing in toxic gases

prematurely exposed to pollution

identified the problem

found a solution

the timing is right plus the execution

a cultural revolution is in progress

full court press

the heat is on

shuffling through the mess

the excess is gone

the pathway is looking clear

the wrong of despair is in repair

the future is finally here

in this present condition

separating fact from fiction

the truth from the lies

a distinct distinction

between the good and the bad guys

the real from the fake

we will not take the bait

won't be strung along

rather wait for change

won't take the con

far from an Uncle Tom

share bonds with Nat Turner

not letting the forces that be

get away with murder

we will not be burglars in the night

staying out of sight

we are guided by the ethereal light

Nazirites

soldier for the cause

fighting for reformation against unjust laws

we will not pause until the litany is through

this is not for reward or applause

but for the embattled many

and chosen few

RIGHTEOUS WAY TO GO

The streets aren't paved with gold

but we are

the legend was told

but attention spans are miniature

misdirected minds blasting off with Kevlar

runaway slaves searching for the North Star

crossing the ravine like Cesar

refugees looking to even the score

nothing passive about our aggressive Eeyore

either or

when seeking for peace we prepare for war

BE THIS WAY

Crime and degradation

jailed minds receive no education

ain't no train waiting for them at the station

only a bus heading upstate

all it take is one mistake

then the jakes on you like jackals

orange jumpsuit with a matching pair of shackles

strapped tight around your wrist and ankles

You have been made an example

the prosecutor requests that years get added onto your sentence

you'll have time for repentance

when you are holding onto your penance

tossed in a cell with disgruntled tenants

Now you labeled a menace to society

a reject of humanity

screaming out profanities

then turn around and ask God please

as each day passes it gets harder to believe

doesn't seem like you'll ever leave

listening to the guard's keys jingle

as they pass your cell

no pleasantries

they don't care if you're doing well

they press you constantly to show and tell

but you keep your mouth closed

because *snitches* get stitches

cancelled

Don't know how much more you can handle

head spinning like a carousel

hope that times flies

to rise from this living hell

getting out is a wet dream like the tears in your eyes

only a thought to sit and dwell

MASK

They are as obvious as the day is bright

thieves and murderers

pimps in chinchilla furs

street hustlers

dealers and customers

called the scourge of the earth,

but there are those that are even worse

those that hide in plain sight

they can be found at work or church

convenient lies

sweet-talk you

into signing over your estate and emptying your purse

it's all in their presentation

they manipulate when they converse

reversing the process of being honest

making you gullible like Forrest

enjoy the thrill of deception

desire to know how far they can go

testing the limits of distrust

DOUBLE-SIDED

There is something happening here

there is change in the air

but the foul stench of fear

it hasn't disappeared

Young lives decimated in Newtown, Connecticut

schools have become a battleground

fragile minds are delicate

however in tragedy there is promise to be found

In India women publicly gang raped

desecration of moral ineptitude

the misogyny of macho machination

man is nothing without woman

Fiscal cliffs rest on top of a mounted inflation of debt

spending sprees unrivaled

leading to uncanny budget cuts

taxes labor on the back of the middle class

furthering the gap between rich and poor

the cynic's solution to escape an economic ditch

is to continually feud over feudal brutal war

diplomacy isn't a misnomer when used for resolution

a political face-lift

because a divided nation needs restitution

Earth excavated of its resources
oceans crying tears of oil
forests brutally stripped naked
wildlife desperately disappearing
but nature still has faith in humanity
generously providing in the midst of tragedy
believing one day we will get it right

GOING THROUGH THE MOTIONS

I can't speak no more

what for

words falling on deaf ears

cockiness a charade for the scared

you can see it in their eyes

the window to their souls filled with lies

can't blame them

lives lived with lighting crashing down like Raiden

raining steadily on where they're staying

permanently staining any chance of hope

cope with copious shortened ropes to hang themselves

promises of a better tomorrow have been shelved

Cinderella turning back to a wench before twelve

sipping on hope that's turned stale

plethora of plans planted to succeed

but execution failed

society's one-track mind derailed

can't justify sky high school loans

laying flat and getting fat off desperation

because of the lack of jobs

entrepreneurs no better

economic instability

issues have not been resolved

modern day slaves to capital

killing for food that's God given

steadily regressing to primitive animals

cannibals devouring apathetic flesh

sending our seeds to fight ill-advised wars

then at home who do we have left

an organized mess

anxiety and panic attacks the result of stress

and for those working

they working more and getting less

every day on the edge of their seats

don't know if they'll have a job tomorrow

living off a flimsy paycheck week by week

this is an unauthorized critique

but most still going through the motions

momentum hit a roadblock

blocked by indecisiveness and fear,

fear that they will never amount to society's standards

total disregard of their own thoughts

mind plays on rewind over and over

body lifeless although living

brain-dead with a pulse

reality is virtual

and they have gone viral

system corrupted by malware

they have crashed

THE VOICE OF A CAPITALIST

Predisposed to rake cash in caseloads

exponential

concurrently *clocking* currency

a public enema for idealistic a-holes

realistically

society controlled by the Dollar, Pound, Pesos, Euros, Yen

Besos

bank blatantly breaking

inflation

creating tracks caking

laid down railroads

Amtrak stacks moving

pressure won't make my associates Whitney Houston

Fuck a cliché

G.O.A.T. hoopen

enriched flower gluten

hula-hooping around stage props

competition been *comped*

play their position

poster dunk

poster children for the 99% whose revolution sunk

to be blunt

mergers and acquisitions my disposition

it was written

born privileged and entitled

no regard for restrictions

propositions politely placate the twice shy once bitten

to sign over their consent to die for monopolistic expeditions

expeditiously being sent out to war torn countries

hungry for demolition

veils been casted

his-story repeats daily

you've all been type-casted

the have and have-nots

the wealthy and you poor miserable bastards

a waste of matter

but you matter as menial labor

dreams deferred

hope will not come later

looking down on the sad state of existence in a luxury sky scraper

rarified air

when I meet my Maker

it'll be in my villa in Jamaica

when you meet your Maker

I'll be standing right here

fear is the greatest weapon

mix that with deception

altering one's perception achieves desired results

despair sets in

believing a contrived enemy is near

skepticism then sets in like a sedative

divide and conquer assault

smart only applies when you're prepared

constituents and I established a contingency plan

character assassinate civilians with heart

this will be a sterile land

fluoride, chemtrails, prescription drug sales

I know you don't understand

common people are the equivalent of junk emails

but every one and everything serves a purpose

your paychecks deposited in your wallets and purses

then goes back to us when you make a purchase

even when you're not at work

you're still at our service

beckon call

we're humanitarians on the surface

but underneath we're crooked like cursive

and the world is our giant mall

ALL ABOARD

DEATH OF A SALESMAN

Death of a salesman

now a product specialist

position has been itemized

relisted

but as long as there's product

someone has to sell it

no matter their title

that's what they're here to do

sell man

to sell man anything and everything

numerous merchandise

make the customer think it's the next best thing to slice bread

got to watch out for their pitch

the best ones have numerous ways to deliver

could call it their bag of tricks

tricking people into swinging for the fences

in this ball game one strike and you're out

but you can have multiple at bats

A good salesman knows how to reinvent himself

a shape-shifter

rebranding

repackage the same old goods

although the item may change

the game stays the same

sell, sell, sell

most work on commission

If no one no buy,

They get no pay
simple as that
however methodology
and modality complex
multilevel marketing
face-to-face
print advertisement
TV commercial
internet banners
cover all bases
aware a good defense
is a better offense
always on the offensive
might come off offensive
but poised with tact
they call it being straightforward
and you're always paying even before sale
because they want your hard earned trust
to trust them with your funds
Always easier to give than get back
refund policy policed
lock up your cash without due process
not before they process your payment
cash
plastic
PayPal
Bitcoin
no checks

but you've been checked off
All about the numbers
better at addition than subtraction
anything less than projected
sickening
reputation takes hit
inevitably a financial crisis
disarray
packaged dreams for profit
become unsold worthless reality
financial depression
then economic hit-men
set up a financial hit
to see the death of it
a deficit
while the death of one salesman is imminent
there are more where they came from
automated programs
capitalistic syndicate
solicit product and merchandise
SPAM

FOR MY PEOPLE

I knew education was key for our survival

been in our roots

tribal

the more we learned in return we became more reliable

our options were viable

making our opposition maniacal

disciples staying in the clear

professing hope as we watch miracles appear

and for those in despair

please become increasingly self-aware

we're not out of danger yet

the coast is not clear

there's a real threat looming

but it's nothing to fear

because the power of one is multiplied by the power to care

what we share is priceless

standing vindicated on the podium

victory for the righteous

any enemy that dares to fight us

attempts will be pious

we are eternal flames

freedom fires

enough is enough

time to thrust ourselves into the sky

never will be slaves to an excuse

we've broken the chain of lies

to continually seek for eternal truth

until the day we die

INNOCENCE LOST

Save our daughters and heal our sons
stop the violence put down the guns

If preachers and nuns can't get them out of the dark and into the sun
then the battle wages on but the war can be won

And no one said it was going to be easy believe me
family matters but this can't be solved simply in a half hour like on TV

Want to give the youth every opportunity to avoid scrutiny
so it's going to take a group effort from parents to adolescent experts

We all got to put in work before our children are buried underneath
      the dirt
from lack of love or being *mirked*

It won't be their fault it'll be blood on our shirt
let's build a network so the kids can see their net worth
collecting the fruits of their labor from mother earth

I can put their struggles in a verse
but dialogue should be open for them to converse
otherwise they'll remain stagnate like a premature birth

They can go from good to better or from bad to worse
our children are our tomorrows we have to put them first

OUTER PLANETARY
IV

Tempo

Life isn't just one way

made of myriad alternates

the exact coordinates to Source coded within

most set course

but fall off their horse short of their destination

looking in all the wrong places

steps retrace it

walking backwards up winding stair cases in mental mazes

while the soul hangs out

waiting with hands out

as we come in somber from our amazing race

the soul's light emblazons the heart emblem

a refreshing referendum

reacquainting us to where we came from

cosmic particles, nutrients, minerals, chromosomes, and cells

ethereal material

Love

the main chemical component

unconditional process of existence

cyclical

scientific and spiritual

one love indivisible

critical for a stable condition

pineal gland picking up extraterrestrial signals

universal tracking system

Clairsentience, clairvoyant, claircognizance, and clairaudience explaining the unexplainable is simple and attainable

discard logic and rational

embrace the magical aspects of life's limitless potential

all of us palpable disciples of truth

letting old paradigms loose

erase the programming that's been taught since a youth

God exists in everyone and everything

we're all offspring of the proof

AFTER DARK

Catch me on the jet set

one of those secrets

the best kept

don't know what to expect

this is real life not no movie

an enigma the definition of abstract

get close and you'll get high off contact

pheromones laced like a d*oobie*

A GAMBLE

Looking for a drop of light in the slight crack of the wall

to taste the rain drops instead of hearing them fall

maybe I'm thinking too big since my resources are small

maybe I'm thinking too much

or not thinking realistically at all

I've been victimized by circumstances

taken risks without incentives

fell short on advances

wanted to touch the moon

but underneath shadows I snuck glances

still believe I can invest in the future

but the past prevented me from taking chances

I haven't ran from life's possibilities

was told average is as good as life gets

but how can it with its majestic sunrises

breathtaking sunsets

I've made my mistakes

but didn't sleep with regrets

didn't want to crawl in place

instead crossed the world with giant steps

to uncover life's secrets

and to once more place my bets

A MOTHER'S NATURE

As life moves continuous like the oceans and the seas

you have been the current that carries me

for when the sun lights up the noon day sky

I can feel your warmth whenever I walk by

seasons change as the wind blows

you've been there for my yesteryears, todays, and my tomorrows

a witness to your moon dancing with stars above

I can rest assure that I'll forever feel loved

although we are different we are one in the same

your compassion pores like an effervescent rain

washing away my pain

in the firmament of love you have quenched my thirst

you are a queen of fertile dreams

you are mother earth

CYCLICAL

Can it be this free radical has transcended from the physical into the metaphysical, riding on the beat sailing on the lyrical. Slide the fader up another decibel, the level of force is centrifugal, united, indivisible flowing into one, cyclical.

Every time I create it feel like I'm high, the paper is my runway to take off, fly into the friendly skies.
The glare in my eyes is stronger than UV rays, that shiny glaze in my retina is the reflection of literature shining from the page.

My thoughts driving on curbs, rampage, result of being let out of the cage, can't settle for mediocrity, a philosopher on level with Plato and Socrates, an accentuation altering alliteration actually.

Astoundingly amazed how my iambic pentameter rivals Shakespeare's plays, straight from the motherland, the beat beats inside of me that beats like African Nyabinghis.

BANDWIDTH

Silently internalizing

meditating while the sun is rising

standing stoic over the horizon

rationalizing your fate

confirming your faith

letting your spirit resonate in space

looking at the reflection in the mirror

and seeing an evolving race

leaving your marks on time

minutes leave residue to trace

body suspended in glass case

delicate

stillness is the predicate

of your unspoken rhetoric

steering your ship into uncharted territory

exploration of new destination mandatory

because life is a journey that can end shortly

dispel the regrets

do not be scared of the unknown

everything in the universe is shared and personally owned

the world is your home

and with connection to Spirit you'll never be alone

THE CITY OF ANGELS

The City of Angels

the night air bathed in *indo*

as the breath of life spreads

across the mountains, valleys, hills, peaks, beaches

native inhabitants of paradise still roam these lands

the desert sands are the ashes of past conquest

frontiers of the wild, wild West

Fresh perspectives are harvested with imagination

the serendipitous ubiquity of laughter

the laid back cool *esé*

as el sol shines through the open arms of the palm trees

illuminating the concrete canvas

where skateboards transform into space shuttles

kicking and pushing towards unknown destinations

tattooed warriors speak of their barrio

brandishing their tribal colors and signs

all children of the Divine one

There is only one L.A.

freeways run like arteries

going in and out

out and in

the freedom to choose

nothing but space and opportunity

riding waves of unity

Hollywood lines a mirage

never endless summer

time is relative

A hostage to hotel California

we don't ever want to leave

all our needs are thoroughly satisfied

I have died and gone to heaven

eternal bliss

divulged beyond the superficiality

and the jilted paradigms of pretentiousness

Nestled in the belly of Gaya

I plead for the innocence of the fault lines

dancing to the rhythm of earthquakes

as the earth shakes and tectonic plates crash

but we are not broken

as angels we continue to rise to soar

in our unscripted reality

magically creating and recreating classical pictures

for our eternal mind

we are Los Angeles

we are the angels that bathe in the sunshine

IT'S OVER

It's about time

that admonition and imposed restrictions part ways

admitting to the truth can be the hardest

forever isn't always what is displayed

reap what you sow--got to take what you harvest

More or less sending an S.O.S

distress signals permanent

Sanskrit symbols

As the wind blows

love died--widowed

Seasons change

Mad things rearrange

Why it got to *be-a-tryst kiddo*

Blame laid down

poured on concrete

where are the rainbow Skittles

colored pebbles are hard to eat

Broken teeth jagged

Body bruised beat ran ragged

Never took off permanently landed

Many have talents that they took for granted

What is--is never how we planned it

NOTHING

I am nothing

but I have everything I need

food from the earth and air to breathe

I am nothing

but I have everything I need

a sense of peace and thoughts to conceive

I am nothing

but I have everything I need

love in my heart and a spirit at ease

I am nothing

but I have everything I need

my faith everlasting in the Divine I believe

ACID RAIN

Skin off fingertips

peel off yesterday

wash away freshness

only skeletons remain

El Sole

Whisked away in a whimsical whirling dervish

traveling beyond the speed of light in multiple multi-verses

beyond the surface

virtual transparency and clarity

vibrating on a higher frequency

we correlate through sacred geometry

stemming from the tree of life

tapping into a higher energy

an entity of light

a star in the night brightening the earth

the last shall be first

and in-between our dreams satisfy our insatiable thirst

immersed in Gaya's birth

interspersed with matter and particles

metamorphosed into minerals

multiplying unequivocal

perception peripheral

centrifugal force is metaphysical

our angles pivotal

I sphere we on the axis

self-aware gains access

a clear address to our nucleus

acquiesce our genetic molecular structure

pyrosequencing the nucleotides order

ut amaris ama

to be loved love

that's our nature

the God gene embedded in our Adams

on the Eve the Creator brought forth conscious thought

conceived by manual labor

eternally connected like the Egyptian ankh

many try to debunk this as a myth

but this been around longer than the planets exist

this is all alchemical

we are the prophetical alchemists

that consists of liquid, solid and air

a revelation of our genesis

that geneticists study this in laboratories for years

While to Sieks, Sairs, Shamans this is common

transferring sacred knowledge like hemoglobin

the nutrient for existence stored in our riboflavin

unlocking the polypeptide bonds to a safe haven of heaven

emanating our auras magnetism

connecting to the Source

our pituitary a conduit for our 3rd eye vision

necessary for our ascended esotericism

as we travel across the agoroth

shrouded in the sacred cloth of a Seraph

through the space time continuum

centered in our equilibrium

God's creations

experience is our curriculum

FLOAT ON

I'm forever moving

traversing the law of physics like Newton

find my target and glue in

while simultaneously removing unnecessary additives

    like gluten

life's a journey haven't come to any sort of conclusion

wish everyone could come along

total inclusion

but until then I'll stay cruising

don't rush me

and I won't rush-yah Putin

But I love how day to day it changes fluid

in all shapes and forms

I find that thought soothing

while lying on beaches with sand warm

palm trees and Caribbean breeze

been on leave so long

that I can't recollect the time I've been gone

in dreams been to Guam

and to places beyond my recollection

found calm in the power of Om

the Divine guiding my direction

who needs a Best Western to rest in

when the earth takes you in her arms

protection

blankets you with her palms a blessing

Eating her fruits ripe and refreshing

coconut milk and mango meat

what a treat

nature's delicatessen

My prize for being the soul contestant coalescing

co-creating my piece of heaven

but this ain't no *Amazing Race*

asked to be forgiven of my transgressions

this is my *Amazing Grace*

every place I've landed

my perception has expanded

interacted with the locals

from peasants to nobles

Our hearts already in tune

didn't need no Pro-Tools

used our bifocals

to see ourselves in each other

when our vision became the focal point

and like joints stay connected

either on or off the record

still get spins

every second

Astral-projecting

continuously traveling throughout the Ethos

strumming away like a violin

while always showing love to my peoples

we all aliens

foreign to our egos

our forays for days a love forum for Eros

peace until I see you again

as we continue down our starry roads

LOVEY DOVEY
V

MORE THAN YOU KNOW

I'll love you more than you'll ever know

sometimes it doesn't show

been high with me

been low with me

when I only had a buck fifty and a bus pass

never knew how long our love would last

seems like yesterday I met you

the first moment I met you

one became two

didn't have to pursue

I knew

we just clicked

real spit

real quick

got real intimate

got into it

permanent

been right by my side

there is nothing to hide

when lost

you're my guide

my dreams you confide in

frequencies vibing

you're vibrant

a God sent

love written all over our face

evident

what we have has no circumference or measurement

all that matters is our enjoyment

our endorsement is our personal validation

my inspiration

with no expiration

only great expectations for the both of us

don't argue or fuss

what we have is cooperation

trust

passion

lust

an infinite appetite

to bathe in our light

eternal internal flames ignite

like fireworks on 4th of July nights

processing each other faster than terabytes

having flights of fancy

being near you makes my atoms antsy

my nucleus is moving rapidly

if love is blind

I can't see

you're just like candy

my Bambi running through the forest of my imagination

an immaculate conception

the model of creation

a celestial divination

drank from the fountain of your youth

witnessing your powers of rejuvenation

why seek for an explanation

found truth

admiration

sincere communication

no complications

pleasant conversations

patience

positive like an affirmation

planning on being here with you for years

permanent vacation

you batten the hatches

while I man the battle station

love is the basis of our foundation

if I may we make one great combination

I'll love you more than you'll ever know

if you look in my eyes you'll see my soul

telling you you're incredible

indelible

lifting our spirits to a higher elevation

SWEET MUSIC

My rhyme has reason

since you've given it meaning

Now the air that passes through my esophagus and larynx

are pro I and us

Life number six

and for me the tone of you coming home is auspicious

We articulate and pronounce each other clearly

the legato rolls off the palate of our tongues to ascent our melody

I exist before you with tongue out of cheek

I exist before you because your rhythm breathes life

      into the words I speak

You are the song to my heart

me--the booming bass to your rainbow-backdrop

Pen leaves permanent mark

words left unsullied

WISH

Wish I were here for you

Wish I was by your side

Wish I played it fair

Wish I never made you cry

Wish I handled things better

Wish I just let you be

Wish I had you forever

Wish I wasn't sorry

                            I wish

REBIRTH

I died twice when I saw you

the first was the death of the old me

and I died again

knowing that one day you would be gone

therefore I am free

to be with you in the now

BAND-AID

We were adhesive

nothing about us was cohesive

playing give and take

hearts fragile and ours were bound to break

this wasn't a mistake

consider it a lesson

the pain we were carrying had to alleviate

surrendering to the constant depression of what is

that never would be

SEASONS

Before we walked off the platform

thought we could work it out

I was all ears whatever you wanted to talk about

there was no amount of attention I wouldn't give

I had consecutive sweets like an executive

open and receptive

but I know how it is

the days are long

the nights even longer

all I wanted to do was put a smile on your face

when you were somber

satisfy your thirst

be your hunger

never had to wonder where I'd be

I ain't Osama

been here for you and me

thought we could make a house into a happy home

you had my GPS knew where I would roam

You,

the quintessential part of any love poem

lost in your love triangle Bermuda

you didn't have to prove anything to me

what did I have prove to *yah*

I knew you were a mover and a shaker

but if you ever wanted to be saved by the bell

I was your AC Slater

my *flava* came from Liberia and Jamaica

would give it to you anytime

never had to wait for later

always expected

never neglected your needs or concerns

was there when your heart ached

when your heart burned

learned so much from each other

why would I have wanted another

saw you as my future children's mother

only being sincere

not telling you what you want to hear

that wouldn't be fair

it was hard for me to share how I felt

most of the time I kept to myself and dealt

but you could always tell when something was wrong

didn't want to sound like a broken record

another sad love song

however moments fade tender

and it's still hard knowing you're gone

MUCH MORE

I don't know what it sound like

but I know what it feel like

Right

real tight

feels light

like walking on air

lost in the moment

Time

not going anywhere

thoughts of having you near

ready to take off

magic carpet ride

revel in majestic sceneries

the most beautiful is you and I

Destiny

you are a soul child

Gentle

the warmth of your smile

Intoxicating

blood laced with perfume

consumed in her radiance

Magnificent
far from naive
admire her innocence
our third eye
detecting our sixth sense
a delightful preference

Intense
the suspense leaves us entrenched
in a world of difference

Deliverance
going the distance
in this instance
can't fight the resistance

Instincts

GOING BLIND

Can I lick your tears

taste your sorrow

as you look in my eyes

and see no tomorrow

EVIDENCE

I never knew you could be so cruel

like the bully in school

played me for the fool

Never cared about my feelings

I blindly searched for meaning

but you hid that

Not revealing your true intentions

a cog in your wheel of deception

needing my vote of confidence like a politician

I never had a chance--dicked me raw with no protection

left me stranded by the waste side

stripped of dignity and pride

I'd rather have died

than knowing I was living a lie

I would ask why

But you made it painfully obvious

I was your fall guy for the years of distrust

for the men treating you as if you were anonymous

And I was the first sucker that came along

do me in first assumed it wouldn't be long

until I do it to you

Couldn't have been more wrong
but you wanted me to feel your pain

If I knew I was dealing with a woman scorned
then I would have removed the thorns
mended the heart that was torn
but you were too far gone
to be redeemed

staring at your reflection in the pond
while your inner voice screams
for self-esteem
The dreams the promises
your previous lovers schemed
left your heart empty like vacant offices

Officers I've been robbed
the femme fatale stole my affection
as soon as I put down my guard
bypassing all my security

Premeditated
surely she'll be on a spree
to gain revenge
she hungry and her blood lust knows no end

I feel sorry for her next victim
you might fit the description
honest, loyal, trusting
that's all she needs to bust in

Wake up months later from your concussion
with no recollection of your abduction
your trail of tears will be the only clue of her existence
the only warning
when you see her keep your distance

ALL GOOD

It's all good

this ain't no rant or rave

lover scorned

world ripped apart or torn

no *War of the Roses*

Real Housewives of Hip-Hop

Dr. Drew or *Nancy Drew* detective mystery

this is what it is

and what is,

is self-respect, dignity, understanding,

love and caring

taking the high road

even if there isn't one

well I'll just make one

in the end all you have is one

one breath

one you

one moment in time

and time ain't on my side

therefore I have to decide

all I can give you is the present

because the past has passed

and we have no future

A PIECE OF

I know you're not lost

only at a loss for words

you've found the right place

but not the right words

Silence can be golden

when body language speaks in volumes

value priceless

your presence converses freely

Self-portrait of the surreal

image immortalized

a picture says a thousand words

and all the words attributed to you say love

If you can feel me then realize

that I've been putting electricity in the air

there is a storm of love coming our way

I have been waiting for you

specifically your existence

patiently waiting for you to arrive by my side

From the dark that surrounds me

you are the sun

illuminating the future

there is no concept of amount

can't place a price on our priceless moments

as we share a ubiquitous joy for the free world to see

Distance attracts a carnal hunger

we can't resist

unrelenting to fight this urge of insatiable passion

Connection solidified by spiritual forces

guiding us through tranquil emotion

while we elude the distraction of human inadequacies

Living on an elevated plane

beyond the reach of monotony

in the sight of passion and desire

BREAKTHROUGH

Life didn't have to be this complicated

dreams dismissed tomorrows confiscated

thoughts convoluted

sense of urgency castrated

apathetically assimilated to complacency

inundated with let's wait and see

walls empty because there are no windows to opportunity,

but love has a way of getting on through

POETICEXPRESSIONISM: GLOSSARY

Poem: Woman Scorned

Dookie earrings: Big, gold and thick hanging earrings

Shank: To stab

Poem: The Voice Of A Capitalist

G.O.A.T.: Greatest of all time

Besos: kisses in Spanish

Comped: give (something) away free, especially as part of a promotion

Poem: Innocence Lost

Mirked: shot

Poem: The City Of Angels

Indo: another name for marijuana

Esé: Basically means homeboy, dog, dude, man, or homes

Barrio: Spanish for neighborhood

ABOUT THE AUTHOR

Charles Williams is a writer who uses poetry to convey personal feelings as a way to heal, grow and connect. He realizes that the human experience is a shared experience, and he conveys this in his poetry. He is a poet without borders and is comfortable with addressing and dealing with a diverse array of topics and life situations. Charles has been writing and performing poetry for over 15 years.

Poeticexpressionism began as a blog where Charles combined his poetry with music. He feels that when you take the beat away from a song the lyrics are still poetry. He also realized that the contribution of the beat adds depth to the lyrics and gives it additional life.

As a modern day *Renaissance Man*, forward thinker and innovator, Charles writes, teaches, performs, coaches, is an entrepreneur, trainer, healer, dancer, host and inspirational speaker. Charles' poetry has been published in *The Women's Group* vol. 2 & 3 and his Haiku's can be found in the *Heart On's Women in ART Calendar*, 1st and 2nd edition. He is also an Emmy award-winning television producer and has written for the *Huffington Post*.

Poeticexpressionism is available for purchase online @ Amazon.com and on his website: solsinmotion.com. For more information about *Poeticexpressionism* and other works contact Charles Williams @ solsinmotion.com.

www.ingramcontent.com/pod-product-compliance
Lightning Source LLC
Chambersburg PA
CBHW070336230426
43663CB00011B/2342